G000093826

PERSONAL BOOKLET

JOURNEYS

Copyright © CWR 2007
Published 2007 by CWR, Waverley Abbey House,
Waverley Lane, Farnham, Surrey GU9 8EP, UK.
Registered Charity No. 294387.
Registered Limited Company No. 1990308.
Reprinted 2008.
Bible reading notes included in this booklet previously
published by CWR in the March/April 2005 issue of
Lucas on Life Every Day, by Jeff Lucas.
The right of Jeff Lucas to be identified as the author of
this work has been asserted by him in accordance with
the Copyright, Designs and Patents Act 1988, sections
77 and 78.
Introduction: Andy Peck. Questions for group
discussion: Jeff Lucas and Andy Peck.
All rights reserved. No part of this publication
may be reproduced, stored in a retrieval system, or
transmitted, in any form or by any means, electronic,
mechanical, photocopying, recording or otherwise,
without the prior permission in writing of CWR.
For a list of our National Distributors visit
www.cwr.org.uk/distributors
Unless otherwise indicated, all scripture references
are from the Holy Bible: New International
Version (NIV), copyright © 1973, 1978, 1984 by the
International Bible Society.
Concept development, editing, design and production
by CWR
Printed in England by Nuffield Press
ISBN: 978-1-85345-438-7

DAILY READINGS: **JEFF LUCAS**
GROUP DISCUSSION QUESTIONS:
JEFF LUCAS AND ANDY PECK

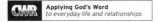

CWR Applying God's Word
to everyday life and relationships

CONTENTS

INTRODUCTION

If you were to examine the prayer topics suggested by members of small groups, concerns about guidance would be high on the list. What should I do about an elderly parent? Which university should I attend and which course? Should I marry my boyfriend? Where should we live? Is it right for me to look to serve overseas? And so members pray for their brothers or sisters, that God might make things clear. Sometimes He does, and we rejoice in His answers. But often He doesn't. Now the group members don't just have the problem of figuring out what to do, they are also wondering where God is in the whole situation!

In these sessions Jeff Lucas encourages us to look at guidance from a completely different angle. It is correct to ask God questions, but maybe we are asking the wrong questions. Are we hung up on the detail when God has some bigger things to show us? Have we spent too much energy looking for the will of God and not enough seeking God Himself?

Let's abandon our ideas about how guidance works and take a fresh look at this whole subject as Jeff shares insights from God's Word: exploding myths, encouraging action and liberating you for a walk with God that is fresh and fulfilling.

How to use

This resource is designed to include all you will need for four small-group sessions. It comprises four DVD clips, group discussion questions based on each clip and Bible readings to be used between each session.

PREPARATION

1. Watch the DVD clip before the meeting.

2. Use the icebreaker to get folk chatting. Select the questions that you think would be most useful for your group to look at. You may want to use them all, depending on the time you have available. We suggest you plan for 30–45 minutes.

THE SESSION

1. Play the DVD clip first and go straight into the icebreaker question.

2. Use the questions you have selected.

3. Move from discussion into prayer. There's a prayer included in the material which you could finish with at the end.

4. Encourage the group to use the daily readings in the days between sessions. The readings expand and build on the topics covered in the DVD. If the group members are not used to daily Bible reading, encourage them to develop this habit. If the group members are already into a routine of Bible reading and prayer each day you might want to discuss how best to work these new readings into their time.

5. You could start the next session by reviewing how the group found the daily readings. What did they learn? Do they have questions to raise? How did God speak?

Session 1:
Confusion for Beginners

ICEBREAKER:
Why is guidance such a tough topic for Christians?
Is guidance an easier or harder topic for people who
aren't believers to understand?

FOR GROUP DISCUSSION:
• How big a role does our temperament play in what
  we look for in guidance? Is having a sense of 'peace'
  important?

• A new Christian tells you that they are feeling
  overwhelmed as they think they need to pray about
  every tiny decision, which is effectively paralysing
  them. What's your advice?

• Do you tend to think of the will of God as a tightrope?
  Is there a second-by-second plan?

• Think back to some of your major decisions in life.
  Have you generally known what to do?

- Why do we think that what we *don't* want to do is probably God's will for us, and what we *do* want is out of His will?

- 'Biblical lucky dip isn't a good idea.' Do you agree?

- Isaiah made himself available for God's purposes. How do we do that?

PRAYER:
Point out the pathway, living God
We are slow to see
Confused at times
Scared to act
Fearful within
And sometimes, believing the worst.

Show us Your ways
Show us Yourself
In Your name.

Amen.

RECENTLY I had the opportunity to visit Niagara Falls, near Toronto, Canada. Displayed there is an old sepia photograph of Blondin, the famous French tightrope walker. He owed his celebrity and fortune to his idea of crossing the Falls on a tightrope 1,100 foot long, 160 foot above the water. Each time he accomplished the feat (first in 1859), it was always with different variations: blindfolded, in a sack, trundling a wheelbarrow, on stilts, carrying a man on his back and sitting down midway while he made and ate an omelette. One faltering step, and he would plummet to his death in the boiling waters below.

I used to think of the will of God as a tightrope – and one which was easy to fall from. I was terrified of the thought of making a mistake and accepting 'second best'. I was paralysed, and almost unable to make any significant decisions.

Since then, I have come to believe that the will of God is much more like a field than a tightrope. There are clear boundaries, but quite a lot of freedom inside those perimeters. In reality, we all live according to the field theory – otherwise we would never confidently make even minor decisions. We realise that God allows us to choose which supermarket to visit, which colour of toothbrush to buy and a host of other decisions in life.

And in the more momentous choices, there is a safety net – it's called grace. Forgiveness and a new start are available to those who stumble. We need to *prioritise* the will of God, but not become *paranoid and fearful* about it. God is bigger than our ability to know and discern His will, and can straighten our paths.

Prayer: Lord, deliver me from a fear of failure: You are great enough to guide me. Help me to rest in that knowledge. Amen.

A field, not a tightrope

BIG PICTURE:
Psalm 43:1–5
Proverbs 3:5–6

FOCUS:
'… in all your ways acknowledge him, and he will make your paths straight.' (Prov. 3:6)

... the will of God

is more like

a field than

a tightrope

Peace is the umpire?

BIG PICTURE:
Colossians 3:15–17

FOCUS:
'Obey what I command you today.' (Exod. 34:11)

'IT'S better felt than telt.' Poor grammar indeed, but that was a saying that went around years ago, suggesting that Christianity is more about being moved emotionally than imbibing information; that it's more about the heart than the head. But I am nervous of the suggestion that truth can be discerned ultimately through subjective feelings, particularly when it comes to knowing the will of God. I was taught if we're in the centre of God's purposes then we'll have a perfect, confirming sense of peace in our hearts. 'The peace acts like an umpire at a cricket match', they said, quoting the Colossians text: 'Let the peace of Christ rule in your hearts…' The idea is that peace is the final confirming nod that we really are doing the right thing.

There are some difficulties with this idea. Firstly, the Colossian text has nothing whatsoever to do with guidance, but is about relationships in the local church. Secondly, feelings are slippery things that can come and go, and relate to diet, tiredness and a host of other factors.

There are times when we feel anything but peace when we make a good decision, particularly if the choice made was in direct conflict with everything that we long for. Then, what matters is not how we feel – what's important is what we know is right, not what feels right; obedience is what counts.

Perhaps the peace/umpire idea came about because we do well not to ignore our conscience, and sometimes feelings of disquiet indicate that this is exactly what we are doing. That said, I'm convinced that my emotional condition makes a poor umpire when it comes to confirming decisions.

Prayer: Lord, I want to walk in peace; but help me to obey You, whatever I feel. Amen.

Forgiveness and a new start are available to those who stumble

REACTING against the teaching that God's will is always painful, difficult, and what we don't want to do, some of us have swung into the opposite extreme – believing that God is just far too nice to disrupt our lives by asking us to do anything that might be awkward or uncomfortable. No, we reason, God's will is just whatever I feel like doing today. Not so. Clearly there *are* times when God has a task that He wants accomplished, and we are invited to accept that mission as our own and get the job done.

Paul's experience of the Spirit of Jesus not allowing him to go into Bithynia and then his night-time vision serves as an example of a life lived under orders. The call to Macedonia was very clear: no debate – don't go here, but go over there, and now! Perhaps it's easier for us when God issues a command like this: there is little doubt about what we are to do; the only question is, will we do it?

All of that said, the fact remains that God still looks for people with willing hearts to do His will rather than fearful conscripts who reluctantly get in line. The call of Isaiah illustrates that well. When I read about that epic day, I can only see God, the angels and Isaiah present – yet the Lord seems to drop a cosmic hint with the booming question, 'Whom shall I send? And who will go for us?' As far as I can see, Isaiah, being the only human there, was the only potential candidate for the task! But God was looking for the offer of availability: 'Here am I, send me.'

Prayer: Lord, count me as one willing to go on the specific missions that You give to me in my life. Amen.

God's will – just what we want to do?

BIG PICTURE:
Acts 16:6–9
Isaiah 6:1–13

FOCUS:
'Then I heard the voice of the Lord saying, "Whom shall I send? And who will go for us?"' (Isa. 6:8)

Surprise,
surprise

BIG PICTURE:
Acts 8:4–8,26–40

FOCUS:
'Who has known the
mind of the Lord?
Or who has been his
counsellor?'
(Rom. 11:34)

ONE of the more dubious 'accomplishments' of the
Church is that we have managed to make God seem
boring. The truth is, He is astonishing. Consistent, He is;
predictable, He is not. Jesus was full of surprises: how
many preachers and teachers launch their ministries at a
party – with a wine miracle? How many of those who pray
for the sick to be healed instruct those who get better
not to tell anyone about what's happened? How many
of the preachers you know will shun crowds rather than
cultivate them?

Craig Barnes puts it well: 'Astonishment is precisely
what is missing in so many of us in the Church today.
We have completed all the fill-in-the-blank Bible study
workbooks and learned all the Christian answers to
questions about every conceivable topic ... the bottom
line is this: if we are not astonished by Jesus, then we are
following something other than the person described in
the Bible.'[1]

The idea that the Lord's purposes for our lives will
always make perfect logical sense is not consistent
with the story of God found in Scripture. Here, Philip
the evangelist is in the middle of a major revival – with
incredible signs and wonders and 'great joy in the city'
– only to be commanded to leave it and go to a deserted
place to meet just one man. That doesn't give us a licence
to be foolish, as though God only ever asks us to do what
seems bizarre. Nonetheless, there are times when what
He asks of us is surprising and even shocking – but when
He does send us on a strange mission, He seems to
speak more emphatically and clearly.

God still looks for
willing hearts to
do His will

**Prayer: Lord, surprise me. Renew my sense of wonder.
Break any boxes that I have built for You. Amen.**

1. M. Craig Barnes, *Sacred Thirst* (Zondervan, 2001).

VISITING the home of a minister friend recently, I noticed that he had a little plaque with a saying on it which at first amused, and then disturbed me. 'If you want to hear God laugh, tell Him your plans.'

Who cares what you think?

Not only does this catchy little slogan suggest that God has complete disdain for what we think and feel – hardly the portrait of a genuinely caring Father – but it is also out of kilter with biblical revelation. Again, surprisingly, God reveals Himself as One who is apparently open to human suggestions – the whole notion of prayer is testimony to the reality that God does want us to share with Him what we think, feel and indeed want from Him. The sight of Moses making prayerful suggestions to the Lord – and God accepting those suggestions – is revolutionary indeed, as it shows God, not as an impassive commanding officer, but One who seems to invite our input.

FOCUS:
'Then the LORD relented and did not bring on his people the disaster he had threatened.'
(Exod. 32:14)

Some years ago, I spent some time asking God for direction because I was considering moving back to the UK from America. Finally, I sensed God saying something to me that shocked me to the core. 'I don't mind – you choose. I'll bless you in either place.' Some readers might recoil as I recount this, but the fact is that God did bless our family – in both places. On this matter, it seemed that being close to God was more important than where we were actually geographically located. God gave us the choice. Do you want to sense that God is listening? Tell Him your plans, your hopes, your dreams. Submit them to Him, but know that they matter to Him.

Prayer: Father, thank You for Your loving, caring interest in the hopes that I have. Amen.

Session 2:
Just Do It

ICEBREAKER:
(You may want to have pens and paper available for this.)
If you were to draw a picture representing how you feel about the words, 'God's will' right now, what would it look like?

FOR GROUP DISCUSSION:
- When you have been confused about a pathway, where have you turned for help? Did you find the help you needed?

- What parts of doing God's will have you found most hard?

- Can you come up with a motto on guidance that expresses your current thoughts about it and how you want to move forward? Eg, 'God's way is always the best way.'

- Why do we sometimes 'wrestle' with God?

• Share your own personal approach to reading Scripture.
  Do you read the Bible daily, with the aid of notes, etc?

PRAYER:
Lord Jesus, You knew what was right, and You did it.
You saw the fight ahead, and You fought it.
You knew what pain was to come, and You took it.
You glimpsed the cross, and You carried it.
You completed the task.
Grant us obedient hearts, that we might fight sin,
Fight complacency, fight temptation,
Fight the tempter, and fight deception.
But grant it, Lord:
May we never fight with You.
Grant us the serenity of surrender.
Amen.

It's all because of grace

BIG PICTURE:
**Romans
1:18–32; 12:1–2**

FOCUS:
'Therefore, I urge you, brothers, in view of God's mercy, to offer ...'
(Rom. 12:1)

IT WAS a familiar enough sound, but this time it stirred fear within me. The gathering roar of the aircraft engines, signalling that we were about to take off on our flight back to the UK, caused me to break into a sweat – and this was no fear-of-flying nervousness. I glanced across at Kay and our two young children, and realised that our relocation back to England was quite a leap of faith; we had no home to go to, no permanent income – just a sense that God had promised to take care of us in this new chapter in our lives. The weight of responsibility lay heavily upon my shoulders. And then I realised: God had clearly signalled His approval of this venture. The burden was not mine alone – His grace was with us as we took off.

Let's affirm again that God gives His power and strength to us to walk in His will – it's all only possible, according to Paul, through His mercy. Earlier in his letter, Paul had painted a dark portrait of the state we were all in before we came to know Jesus – a life spent bringing gladness to God was way beyond our reach, because 'those controlled by the sinful nature cannot please God' (Rom. 8:8).

Yet, we 'who were at one time disobedient to God have now received mercy' (Rom. 11:30). If it were not for that mercy, we would still be following our own path, captive to sin, experiencing the dead-end treadmill of life, without hope or purpose. Grace enables us to walk in God's purposes. It's not just about us being able to get it right: He will help us know and do His will.

Prayer: Lord, I'm glad that I'm not left to my own resources when it comes to following You. Your help is mine. Amen.

I HAD an aunt who was a passionate fan of watching wrestling on the television. Every Saturday afternoon she used to settle herself down next to her somewhat nervous husband. When the match began, she became a transformed woman, her quiet demeanour was sent packing and replaced by screaming and cheering. She would get so absorbed that occasionally my poor uncle would end up in a half nelson. Most matches would end when the stronger wrestler twisted the other's limbs into such contortions that (finally) the weaker one would submit. My uncle would breathe a prayer of thanks as the grappling ended for another week.

Walking in the will of God is sometimes a struggle, but it's not supposed to be a fight where, exhausted and unable to resist anymore, we finally yield and submit reluctantly, our heads bowed in defeat.

Rather, we happily submit – and one reason for that is because obeying God makes perfect sense. A better translation than 'this is your spiritual act of worship' would be 'this is your reasonable, logical service' – a truth that we should remind ourselves of often. The notion that the 'just do your own thing' life is a philosophy that leads to wonderful liberation is far from the truth. Independence from God isn't a good idea at all. Those who choose to ignore His commands quickly discover that sin is a harsh taskmaster, and that rebellion brings disaster. Walking with God produces joy: it's what we were designed for. Put crudely, walking in the will of God is a great deal for us! One translation of our Focus verse says, 'this is what sensible people do.'

Prayer: Father, walking with You works. It's the reason I was born. Thank You for designing and making me for Your purposes. Amen.

Delightful, logical submission

BIG PICTURE:
Romans 12:1–2
James 4:7
Psalm 81:11

FOCUS:
' … offer your bodies as living sacrifices, holy and pleasing to God – this is your spiritual act of worship.'
(Rom. 12:1)

Grace enables us to walk in God's purposes

We *can* please God

BIG PICTURE:
Romans 12:1–2
Psalm 149:1–9
Zephaniah 3:17

FOCUS:
'... holy and pleasing to God ...' (Rom. 12:1)

A FRIEND of mine works in the pressure-cooker environment that comes with being a car salesman. Every day for him is a race to meet the quota and hit the ever higher sales targets that his employers set each month. But even when all the targets are hit, the owner of the company has a habit of calling each month to 'chew everyone out' as my friend puts it. 'He believes in keeping us scared – even when we've done our best and sales are sky high, his philosophy is that we can always do better – hence the monthly verbal roasting.'

The sad reality is that employees won't last long in such a negative environment – no one can survive in a continual atmosphere of discouragement forever.

Many Christians serve a God who is more like an eternally discontented boss than a loving heavenly Father. As far as they're concerned, no matter how much they pray, study, resist sin and tell others about Jesus, it just won't be good enough for their God. He is never pleased. That leads to paranoia about the will of God – even when good choices are made, God, they think, probably isn't impressed. After a while, they begin to wonder why they bother.

The God of the Bible is frequently described as being pleased with us, particularly by Paul in his writings (Rom. 14:18; Col. 3:20). Even though we continue to be imperfect people who are still in the process of sanctification, we are *holy* – set aside for God's purposes – and a source of delight to Him. Zephaniah paints a picture of the God who dances with joy over us – a great reason to continue to pursue His will.

Prayer: Lord, today I want to be more than an efficient, productive or even successful person. I want to please You. Amen.

THE urge to fit in with the crowd is very strong for all of us. The multi-billion-pound fashion industry (more money is now spent worldwide on advertising than on education) relies totally on that herding instinct that seems to drive us to want to be similar to each other. Sometimes the results are bizarre. Currently as I write there is a trend to wear jeans so low-slung that the elastic waistband of your underwear is clearly shown. This 'fashion' was started by inmates in prisons who are not allowed belts, so they have adopted an enforced low slung look. Without thinking why we do what we do, we long to belong.

But the Christian is, by nature, a non-conformist. As followers of Jesus we have decided to march to a different drumbeat; nevertheless we are still aware that the world urgently demands that we get in step with a rhythm that is contrary to God's will. Our minds are bombarded daily by a distorted value system. The Germans call this dominating, prevailing philosophy the *zeitgeist* or 'spirit of the age'. But those who want to do the will of God have to realise that choosing God's purposes will invariably involve us in having to desert the crowd sometimes. Living in the world, we are nevertheless no longer 'of the world' (John 17:15–16).

But Paul is not advocating escapism here; his call that we 'come out from them and be separate' mustn't prompt us to try to shut ourselves off from the world. Instead, we live totally in the world, yet refuse to get in line and follow the pied piper that is the spirit of the age. And that takes grace.

Prayer: Lord, I want to follow You, not the confused, misguided voice of the world today. I need Your grace. Amen.

Don't just go
with the flow

BIG PICTURE:
Romans 12:1–2
2 Corinthians 6:14–7:1

FOCUS:
'Do not conform any longer to the pattern of this world …'
(Rom. 12:2)

We are …

a source of

delight to Him

Transformation and renewal

BIG PICTURE:
Romans 12:1–2
Ephesians 4:17–24
Colossians 3:1–11

FOCUS:
'... but be transformed by the renewing of your mind.' (Rom. 12:2)

... we need to guard carefully what we put into our minds

THE telephone call was cut short by the sound of a piercing scream. Happily, no one was being murdered – but the chap on the other end of the line had realised that the multi-tasking of filling his tank with petrol *and* participating in a conference phone call had led to a disaster. He had filled his (petrol) car with diesel. The pumps are helpfully marked to prevent such calamity – the diesel nozzles are wrapped in sombre black plastic. This should be a strong warning that we are likely to give our cars major indigestion if we should happen to put the wrong stuff in. Recklessly, my hapless friend went ahead – with perilous results. The car engine was not amused. It choked.

If we want to walk in the will of God, we need to guard carefully what we put into our minds. A healthy mind is a key, not only to discerning direction, but to any potential growth in our Christian lives. The word translated 'transform' here is the root of the word 'metamorphosis'. It describes a gradual change from within. True growth for the disciple of Jesus does not just come as we alter our outward behaviour, because it's possible to perform the right acts outwardly but still have a heart that is unchanged. This was the trap into which the Pharisees of Jesus' day fell (Matt. 23:27–28).

A healthy mind is also like a compass when it comes to decision-making. When we fill our thinking with smeared images and profane words, our ability to make good choices about what is right and wrong will be eroded. We read in Proverbs, '... guard your heart, for it is the wellspring of life' (4:23).

Prayer: Lord, there's so much corrosive and dangerous material with which I can fill my mind.

Session 3:
How God speaks

ICEBREAKER:
If you could ask God anything and know you would receive an instant answer, what would you ask?

FOR GROUP DISCUSSION

- How does God most commonly make His ways known to you?

- How can our friends help us to discern the voice of God?

- What other methods has God used to speak to you?

- Were any particularly memorable?

- Why do you think God often makes us wait for answers?

- Have you experienced God speaking to you through 'prophetic' statements made by others?

- How can we know if a dream has come from God, or merely from our own imaginations?

- Does God have something to say to us about everything?

- Has God ever let you know that He was happy to leave a specific decision to you?

- How do we get wisdom?

PRAYER:
Thank You, Lord, for You are not silent.
Give us ears to hear, that we may learn to recognise
the sound of Your voice.
Teach us how to learn, from Your Word,
and from our own ways
That wisdom might be ours.
Make us to be people of discernment
Who know Your voice
Who love Your voice
Who listen
And who obey.
Speak, Lord.
Your servants are listening.
Amen.

WE WERE on a family day out, and I was very eager to find the sea. I pulled the car over and asked a friendly-looking elderly pedestrian if he could tell us where the beach was. He looked stunned. We were actually driving down the promenade, so everything to our right was a vast expanse of blue ocean. I was asking for directions to find something that was hugely obvious. He marvelled at what was either my stunning stupidity or my acute lack of observational skills. Pointing to the crashing waves, the pedestrian smiled and advised me never to become a detective. 'Gathering evidence would be a challenge for you, son.'

Sometimes we go to God asking questions about His will, but the solution is already right there in front of us, contained in God's Word, the Bible. We need look no further, and seek no additional confirmation. That means that we don't have to fret and wonder about whether or not we should steal, commit adultery, gossip or be unkind. God has already spoken, and He isn't about to change His mind.

In some areas of the Church, there seems to be a greater emphasis on prophecy and the gifts of the Spirit than on the value of good, biblical teaching. While I am personally completely committed to the right use of those wonderful gifts, this should not be at the expense of ensuring that we have a solid biblical foundation, both as we study and reflect privately, and as we hear public teaching. Don't go looking for oceans that are already right in front of you.

Prayer: Lord, thank You for the clarity I find in Your Word. Help me to build right foundations in my life.

The foundation of the Bible

BIG PICTURE:
2 Timothy 3:16–17

FOCUS:
'All Scripture is God-breathed ...' (2 Tim. 3:16)

Sometimes ...

the solution

is right there

in front of us

Wisdom and maturity

BIG PICTURE:
Ephesians 4:1–15

FOCUS:
'Like newborn babies, crave pure spiritual milk, so that by it you may grow up in your salvation, now that you have tasted that the Lord is good.' (1 Pet. 2:2–3)

WHEN our children were very small, they asked us about almost every decision. Could they go out and ride their bikes? Was a bar of chocolate on the menu? How about an ice cream? Every day was filled with delightful enquiries about details. That's all changed: both our children are grown up now – so I don't expect my son to call me to ask permission to ride his bike. Part of growing up means that responsibility to make many decisions is now devolved.

It seems that as we grow in wisdom, God allows us some freedom to make good choices. The New Testament gives a number of examples. Paul writes to the Corinthians about the issue of going to meals where food has been offered to idols – and although he gives some broad principles, he also says 'If you want to go …' (1 Cor. 10:27–29). We're also encouraged to make sound decisions about giving (2 Cor. 9:7), aspirations about leadership (1 Tim. 3:1) and the choice between marriage and celibacy (1 Cor. 7:8–9).

I'm astonished sometimes at the immaturity and lack of wisdom that some of us show when we make decisions. We've all met those people whom 'God has called to sing', seeing as He 'gave them a song'. Without being unkind, we hear the tune and conclude that perhaps God gave it to them because He didn't want it. When one is called to function in an area of gifting, we can assume that the basic gift will be in place as a confirmation of that call. Gaining and developing wisdom will save us – and others around us – a lot of pain.

Prayer: Father, I want to grow up and be a Christian of genuine maturity. Give me a clear mind and a wise heart. Amen.

THE story of the call of Samuel has an almost humorous, Monty Python feel about it. Young Samuel heard such a clear sound that he repeatedly mistakes God's voice for that of Eli – and goes backwards and forwards waking the old priest up until Eli finally realises that the Lord is doing the speaking. Eli had enough wisdom to tell Samuel how he should position himself before the God who speaks; an attitude of openness and availability was an important prerequisite: '… say, "Speak, LORD, for your servant is listening."' God speaks to those who want to hear and obey what He says – His servants.

I've never had an experience of hearing the *audible* voice of God, but have met people who have. Without fail, they were utterly changed by the encounter – just as those who heard that voice in the Bible were never quite the same again. Adam, Moses, Elijah, Isaiah, Ezekiel, Peter, James and John, Paul and, of course, Jesus, all heard the audible voice of the Father.

To hear Him speak like that is no light thing – the word 'voice' in the Old Testament usually means 'thunder'. Again, those who seem constantly to 'hear voices' concern me – biblically, these encounters were not everyday experiences about trivial matters, but were epic, life-altering moments that would be burned upon the hearer's memory for all their days. So – you and I may have an experience of hearing God in that way, but if we haven't, we shouldn't take that as a reason to worry about our spirituality. Perhaps God reserves those incredible moments for a few, and then only occasionally in their lives does He speak audibly.

Prayer: Lord, however You will do it, please speak to me; not to entertain or thrill me, but to change me. Amen.

The audible voice of God

BIG PICTURE:
1 Samuel 3:1–21

FOCUS:
'Then the LORD called Samuel.' (1 Sam. 3:4)

God speaks
to those who
want to hear
and obey …

Dreams and visions

BIG PICTURE:
Numbers 12:3–6
Judges 7:9–15

FOCUS:
'And afterwards, I will pour out my Spirit on all people. Your sons and daughters will prophesy, your old men will dream dreams, your young men will see visions.'
(Joel 2:28)

MY GRANDMOTHER had resisted all my attempts to share the gospel with her. She wasn't hardhearted – just one of those incredibly kind, selfless people, who didn't appear to be much of a sinner in need of saving. She'd told me that she was coming to church the next day. I was preaching, and obviously hoped something would impact her.

That night I had a dream, and heard a voice saying repeatedly, 'there is a broad way and there is a narrow way'. Sensing that the Holy Spirit was speaking, I changed my sermon to include that text. My grandmother looked indifferent to the service and the preaching until I reached the point where I quoted the 'broad way' text – when she immediately burst into tears, and gave her life to Christ at the end of the meeting. The dream had contained a key to her heart.

Not every dream comes from God; and Christians are often nervous about hearing God through dreams because of New Age practices; yet from Genesis to Revelation, dreams and visions have been a vital means of God's communication with humankind. Dreams and visions were a chosen way for God to lead, warn, prepare, comfort and encourage His people. Whether it be Jacob, Joseph, Gideon, Daniel, David, Solomon, Job, Isaiah, Jeremiah, Ezekiel, Amos, Zechariah, Joseph, Paul, Cornelius, Pilate's wife, Peter or the unparalleled visions of John the Revelator, God got the attention of all of them through words and pictures that came in daylight or darkness. Don't try and turn a dream that was inspired by late-night cheddar into a mighty revelation – yet don't dismiss those impacting, clear and oft-repeated dreams either.

Prayer: Lord, take charge of my waking and sleeping moments. Be Lord of my dreams; if it is Your will, speak through them to me. Amen.

THE voice was familiar – dear old George stood up to 'prophesy' every Sunday morning; the problem was, he always said the same thing, invariably had a quivering voice and always prefaced his outbursts with the statement 'Thus says the Lord'.

Certainly, not everything that is declared as 'prophecy' really is. Nonetheless, it is obvious from reading Scripture that God often chooses to speak to us through the lips of others – in prophecy, which, by the way, is not always about foretelling the future, but is mostly to do with *forth-telling* truth. Prophecy is a gift that is used by the Holy Spirit to create those red letter days when vital decisions are made; the church in Caesarea had women who prophesied (Acts 21:9) and Paul received a very dramatic prophecy about his future.

Personally, my life has been impacted repeatedly by the gift of prophecy; the ministry I now function in, the house that I live in and the specifics of much of what I do have all come about as a result of prophecy. But let me offer some words of gentle caution too. Sometimes prophecy can be used in a manipulative manner to control and direct inappropriately. Prophecy should generally only confirm what we are already sensing God would have us to do.

And while I believe in the biblical reality of personal prophecy – where someone shares something directly with us (we see Agabus doing that in Caesarea with Paul) – we should avoid *private* prophecy, where we are told not to share what has been said to us with others. Tell trusted confidants the contents of any prophecy given to you: they can help you in that weighing and evaluation that is so vital.

Prayer: Father, help me to be open to the prophetic – both to me and through me. Amen.

Prophecy

BIG PICTURE:
Acts 21:7–16
1 Corinthians 14:26–40

FOCUS:
'Therefore ... be eager to prophesy ...'
(1 Cor. 14:39)

God often chooses to speak to us through the lips of others

Session 4:
Stop Looking for the Will of God

ICEBREAKER:

'What do you want to do when you grow up?' When you were young and were asked this question, what did you say? Did you end up doing what you thought you would? Why?

FOR GROUP DISCUSSION

• 'Stop looking for the will of God.' How do you react to this statement?

• Why are some of us uncomfortable with silence?

• How can we develop more 'Selah' moments?

• Are you clear about where you are heading in life? How could you become more certain?

• Jesus had to actively choose the will of God – it didn't come automatically. Think of His life as described in the Gospels. What practices helped Him to choose God's will?

- Do you think that God speaks more clearly and loudly to newer Christians than to those who have been in the faith for a while? If so, why?

- Character development doesn't happen overnight.
  Is there an area in your life where you would like to see improvement? If you are comfortable to share this, tell the group about it so they can pray for you.

PRAYER:
Lord, we ask not just for blessing: give us You.
Lord, we ask not just for protection: let peace be ours as we know we are at Your side.
Lord, we ask not just for provision, but for the rest that is from knowing You as our Provider.
Lord, we ask not just for guidance, but for a greater knowledge and love for You as our Guide.

God, we long for You.

Amen.

Willingly embracing an uncomfortable future

BIG PICTURE:
Luke 1:26–35

FOCUS:
'For I have come down from heaven not to do my will but to do the will of him who sent me.'
(John 6:38)

WHAT would it be like to be incredibly rich, only to make a decision to turn your back on days spent in sheer luxury, and willingly determine to trek uphill on a harder pathway? I recently met a man who has made that choice. A missionary to Haiti, he comes from an extremely wealthy family that has totally disowned him because of his choice to follow Jesus. Now he has come to a place where 'stuff' doesn't matter much. His tiny home in the hills has neither electricity nor water, so friends brought him a generator – which he has since given away to the local village where he serves; 'I can go to bed when it gets dark. They need it more.' It's one thing to say 'Your will be done' when you have no real idea what changes that prayer might usher into your life – but my friend has stared the implications of his choices in the face and has still decided to be faithful.

Jesus did the same. We can only imagine what the glories of heaven must have been like for the Son who has forever been the Father's delight. Scripture declares that 'he was rich'. Yet, the wonder of it is that He then chose to become poor (2 Cor. 8:9). There came a day when He left the harmonies of angel song far behind him, coming to earth's squalor to be born of a virgin. Perhaps the angels burst into song before the shepherds partly because they missed serenading the darling of heaven. And then it was onward, resolutely, to that bloodied Calvary hill. He chose, even when He knew exactly what the choice meant.

Prayer: Lord, help me to make good decisions when I know full well they will be very costly. Amen.

MOST successful corporations are able to sum up their mission statement in one or two short, pithy sentences. So, in 1990 the Wal-Mart Corporation announced what they were about: 'To become a $125 billion company by the year 2000.' The Sony Corporation are now one of the world leaders in electronics production – but they affirmed back in the pre-computer age of the 1950s that they would 'become the company most known for changing the worldwide poor-quality image of Japanese products'. And then 3M, who gave us the genius of 'Post-it' notes, define their reason for existence: 'To solve unsolved problems innovatively.'

Each of these organisations has been able to get to the point about what they are about; and we would do well to emulate them. It would be good if we could sometimes describe God's will for our life with a specific stroke instead of broad generalisations. Can we say in a sentence what we think our main contribution to life on this planet is to be? And let's not be vague: 'to glorify the Lord' won't work, noble as it sounds. Just how do we plan to glorify Him? Do we have family mission statements? What are *we* about?

Jesus understood clearly what He was to do and could articulate that mission statement easily. He came to bring freedom, and was able to read the Jubilee scriptures, close the book, and say, 'This is it.'

Of course, mission statements are only useful if we actually live by them. Jesus announced freedom time – and then, in the synagogue, set a demonised man free. Why are you here? And then, to quote the Nike Corporation, *'Just do it.'*

Prayer: Father, show me my purpose, and help me to prioritise and choose as a result of knowing why I am here. Amen.

Get to the point

BIG PICTURE:
Luke 4:14–36

FOCUS:
'… I love the Father and … I do exactly what my Father has commanded me.' (John 14:31)

Mission

statements are

only useful if we

actually live

by them

Character
formation and
the will of God
BIG PICTURE:
Luke 5:12–16
Romans 8:29

FOCUS:
'Anyone who has seen
me has seen the Father.'
(John 14:9)

HAVE you ever met Christians who are holy in the worst possible way? One would have expected that their alleged close proximity to God (they pray a lot, and read the Bible more) would make them kinder, more generous people. Tragically, in some cases people develop a holiness that is shrivelled, mean and unattractive. They move from being confident to being bigoted. We look at them and deduce if that's what spirituality does to a person, carnality is rather attractive.

Of course, a person who truly walks with God will become more like Him; but let's not reduce being in the will of God to us merely fulfilling certain tasks. A major part of God's plan for us is that we be 'conformed to the image of the Son'.

Jesus came to serve the Father – and show the Father's nature through His own life and character. Throughout the Gospels, Jesus reiterated that He never did anything aside from that which He saw the Father doing – and that He did nothing except that which the Father told Him to do. So here, Jesus' actions and statements to the leper were echoing what was going on in God the Father's heart. His Father was compassionate and caring – and Jesus was too.

It is impossible to walk in the will of God for our lives and not somehow manifest the character and nature of the Father. Obviously, Jesus uniquely and exclusively revealed the Father; nonetheless we are all invited to allow the Holy Spirit to form godly character in us. The statement 'Don't look at us, look at Jesus', just won't work – He is currently invisible. The Father wills that we live as those who reflect His beauty.

Prayer: Lord, I want to be like You, so that when people meet me today, they will catch a glimpse of what You are like. Amen.

WE USED to live next door to a lady who hated Christians with vehement passion. She was not shy; sometimes she would lean out of her window and 'greet' me when I pulled up outside the house. The street would be filled with her screamed expletives as she announced to the neighbourhood that the 'blank blank minister' from the 'blank blank church' was in the area yet again. (She didn't actually use the word 'blank', if you get my drift …)

I realised that there wasn't much I could do to win her; some unknown wounding in her history had probably led her to decide that Christians were worthless. Perhaps someone who professed to love God had betrayed or disappointed her; loud bitterness was the fruit of that bruising.

It is God's will that we try to be a blessing to others whenever we can; certainly that's how Jesus, the Servant King lived, and it's what He taught His followers to do – they were to be distributors of peace wherever they went. I keep hearing about people who have decided not to use builders or tradespeople who are Christians because some have a reputation for doing a poor job, being late and overcharging. Whatever else this is, it's certainly not the will of God for Christians to run their businesses in this way.

Not everyone will be won over in a world that has a tendency to hate God and His people (Mark 13:13). But that shouldn't stop us from aspiring to be those who enjoy 'a good reputation with outsiders' (1 Tim. 3:7). How wonderful it would be if the people who live in our towns were grateful because we live there too.

Prayer: Help my words, thoughtfulness and practical actions to make a positive impression on others today. Bring peace through me. Amen.

Becoming a blessing

BIG PICTURE:
Luke 10:1–12

FOCUS:
'They broke bread in their homes and ate together with glad and sincere hearts, praising God and enjoying the favour of all the people.' (Acts 2:46–47)

We discover

who we are …

through our daily

relationship with

the Father

SESSION 4: DAY 5

Willing to be interrupted

BIG PICTURE:
Luke 18:15–17, 35–43

FOCUS:
'Trust in the LORD with all your heart and lean not on your own understanding; in all your ways acknowledge him, and he will make your paths straight.' (Prov. 3:5–6)

EVER noticed just how 'organised' life has become these days? People used just to 'drop by' at each other's homes; it still happens occasionally, but some of that joy has been eroded by the filofax-driven culture that we now live in. Planning a nice meal with friends is now more likely to involve consulting a palm pilot, a notebook computer or (if you're really sensible) an old-fashioned paper diary that you actually write things in. The sad reality is that we can resolutely march through life, oppressed by the rapidly approaching horizon of deadlines that we know we won't meet; efficient, preoccupied, and consumed by our own agendas.

Jesus lived the most significant life that has ever been lived, yet in walking in His Father's will He was willing to make room for those serendipitous moments that others wanted to dismiss as interruptions. Today's reading contains two examples of times He was interrupted by people who were not considered too important in the society of the day – children and a beggar.

It seems that Jesus frequently allowed 'interruptions' – at the marriage at Cana (John 2:4–8), at the feeding of the five thousand (John 6:1–12) and the healing of the man who was born blind (John 9:1–7).

God can direct our paths without advising us that He is doing so. Those 'happy coincidences' where we just seemed to be at the right place at the right time can be the result of God helping organise our steps to make us a source of blessing to others. So look out for those unexpected, unplanned twists in the road. You may just be walking into an appointment that God made for you.

... Jesus

frequently

allowed

'interruptions' ...

Prayer: Father, surprise me, interrupt me, help me to be open to what I had not planned, but what You may have in store. Amen.